CW01082884

Original title:

The Intimate Art

Author: Sebastian Sarapuu

ISBN HARDBACK: 978-9916-89-178-0

ISBN PAPERBACK: 978-9916-89-179-7

ISBN EBOOK: 978-9916-89-180-3

# Tapestry of Touch

Fingers entwined in the night,
Whispers weave through the dark,
Every caress, a soft flight,
Creating paths, leaving a mark.

Textures blend in the air,
Silken threads of warm sighs,
Moments captured, vivid and rare,
In the dance where silence lies.

Skin glimmers in the glow,
Heartbeat mirrors the strife,
As shadows fade, feelings grow,
Stitching love into life.

Colors merge, spirits soar,
Crafted hearts, a gentle seam,
Under stars, we explore,
Life's intricate, waking dream.

In each touch, worlds collide,
Fragile yet boldly they bloom,
Together, we joyfully stride,
In this crafted, shared room.

# Embers of Desire

In the glow of dusky light,
Flickers dance, igniting deep,
Passions rise, hearts take flight,
In the heat, secrets we keep.

Lips linger, tasting the fire,
Eyes lock in daring embrace,
Every moment stokes the desire,
Euphoria lingers in space.

Breathless whispers fill the dark,
Electricity flows in the air,
Each touch ignites a spark,
A tantalizing game we share.

Time suspends in tender gleam,
As shadows paint our skin's plea,
Caught in the pulse of a dream,
Two souls burning, wild, and free.

Embers glow, unforgettable trail,
Weaving tales of lust and want,
In the warmth, we set sail,
In desires that forever haunt.

# Echoes in the Quiet

In whispers soft, silence blooms,
Memories float like dust in light,
Each heartbeat gently resumes,
We dance through shadows of night.

Footsteps trace familiar grounds,
Lingering tones linger here,
In the stillness, love resounds,
Echoes of voices so near.

Fragments of laughter replay,
As the world fades to a sigh,
Moments cherished, never fray,
Each tenderness, a lullaby.

In the quiet, dreams take flight,
Carried by the softest breeze,
Wrapped in warmth, hearts ignite,
Finding solace, sweet release.

Through the hush, connections weave,
Ties of spirit intertwine,
In the echoes, we believe,
Unity in the divine.

## Heartbeats on the Page

Ink flows like blood through veins,
Words dance in a rhythmic grace,
Each heartbeat a story contains,
Captured in time and space.

Pages turn, tales untold,
Whispers of love, joy, and tears,
In the margins, dreams unfold,
Every line, a glimpse of years.

Fingers trace the printed lines,
A pulse felt, with each embrace,
Every letter, feeling shines,
In this vast, eternal place.

Memories etched in careful thought,
Sketching paths where we have strayed,
In these words, the heart is caught,
The soul's journey, lovingly laid.

With every chapter, life ignites,
A tapestry of hopes and fears,
Books alive with heartbeats' lights,
Witness to our laughter and tears.

# Emblems of Longing

Upon the window, raindrops dance,
Whispers of dreams, a fleeting glance.
Hearts entwined in shadows cast,
Yearning echoes from the past.

Beneath the stars, a silent plea,
Winds of change, setting hearts free.
In every sigh, a tale unfolds,
A story of love, forever told.

With every breath, the night feels warm,
Gentle hands, a soft alarm.
Hope ignites in the stillness,
A flicker amidst the chillness.

Moments stolen, time stands still,
Sipping dreams from a magic quill.
Emblems of longing fill the air,
Hearts that know, hearts that care.

In twilight's glow, we find our way,
Guided by love, night turns to day.
With every heartbeat, fate aligns,
Emblems of longing, love defines.

## Silhouettes of Desire

In shadows cast by the setting sun,
Silhouettes of desire, two as one.
Stolen glances, electric air,
What we crave, we lay bare.

Fingers brush in twilight's embrace,
Time slows down in a sacred space.
Every heartbeat, a whispered call,
In the silence, we risk it all.

Moonlit nights and tangled sheets,
In your gaze, my world repeats.
Every secret, every sigh,
In the dance, we won't deny.

With every touch, the flames ignite,
Lost in the warmth of the night.
Silhouettes of desire float free,
In this moment, it's you and me.

As dawn approaches, colors blend,
In the light, our dreams descend.
Together we rise, hearts in flight,
Silhouettes of desire, pure delight.

# Intimacy in Ink

Pages flutter, the scent of dreams,
Words in shadows, soft moonbeams.
Every letter, a whispered truth,
Ink spills secrets of lost youth.

With every stroke, emotions flare,
Intimacy found in the air.
A story written, heart laid bare,
In quiet corners, love we share.

Tales of passion, fears and hopes,
Ink weaves destinies with ropes.
In ink-stained hands, the future shines,
A canvas of love, where light entwines.

Echoes linger on the page,
Revealing every hidden stage.
Intimacy flows, a sacred thread,
Binding us close, wherever we tread.

As chapters close, new ones start,
Every word, a piece of heart.
Intimacy in ink, our legacy,
A love story, wild and free.

## Choreography of Feelings

In the space between our souls,
A dance unfolds, as love consoles.
Steps of longing, twirls of grace,
Choreography of feelings, we embrace.

With every movement, stories blend,
A rhythm shared that will not end.
Footprints left on hearts so bare,
In the silence, our secrets share.

The world fades, it's just us two,
In this pas de deux, dreams come true.
Silent vows in each embrace,
A dance of love, time can't erase.

As music swells, we find our way,
Every heartbeat, a gentle sway.
In the spotlight, our spirits soar,
Choreography of feelings, we explore.

With every leap, the stars align,
Lost in this moment, you are mine.
A dance forever, hearts intertwined,
Choreography of feelings, love defined.

# The Quiet Bloom

In the stillness of dawn's embrace,
Petals unfurl with gentle grace.
Whispers of color, soft and sweet,
Nature's promise beneath our feet.

Dewdrops linger on silken threads,
Echoes of light where silence spreads.
A fragrance dances on the breeze,
Carrying secrets from the trees.

Among the shadows, beauty thrives,
In hidden corners, still it strives.
In quiet moments, we can find,
The blooming heart of peace combined.

Every bud tells a silent tale,
Of resilience found in a gentle gale.
In twilight's glow, the colors blend,
A quiet bloom, where lives transcend.

So take a breath, let nature sing,
In every silence, joy takes wing.
Embrace the calm, let worries fade,
In the quiet bloom, our hearts are made.

# Eclipsed Hearts

In shadows cast by love's embrace,
Two souls entwined in a hidden space.
Waves of longing, soft and deep,
In eclipsed moments, secrets keep.

With every glance, a spark ignites,
Painting the dark with tender lights.
An orbit drawn by unseen fate,
In whispered breaths, we dissipate.

The world can watch as we collide,
In silence whispers dreams abide.
Through moonlit nights, our spirits soar,
In this eclipse, we crave for more.

Time dances slow in the quiet glow,
While hopes and fears begin to flow.
In the spaces where shadows start,
We find our way, two eclipsed hearts.

So let the stars weave our tale,
Through every twist, we will prevail.
In the dark, we'll find our light,
Eclipsed hearts shining, ever bright.

# A Symphony of Us

In perfect harmony, we find our way,
A symphony of love, come what may.
Each note a whisper, soft and clear,
In this grand orchestra, you are near.

Like rivers flowing, our melodies blend,
Through every storm, our song won't end.
The rhythm of hearts, a delicate dance,
In twilight's glow, we take our chance.

With every heartbeat, a new refrain,
Together we rise, through joy and pain.
In the silence, our souls align,
A masterpiece crafted, truly divine.

The echoes of laughter, the tears we share,
Composing a love that's beyond compare.
In the symphony of dreams we weave,
A tapestry of hope, we believe.

So let the world play its part and see,
The canvas of life, just you and me.
In every crescendo, we'll trust the muse,
Together forever, a symphony of us.

## Sculpting the Invisible

Whispers of dreams, in shadows they dwell,
Molding the silence, where feelings swell.
With hands soft as dusk, we trace the night,
Crafting the unseen, from darkness to light.

Thoughts like clay, reshaped with each breath,
Chiseled by moments, of love and of death.
In every curve echoes a tale untold,
A canvas of heartbeats, both fragile and bold.

Fingers entwined, we shape what's not seen,
Bridging the void where the soul's ever keen.
In spaces between, where time feels the same,
Breath of the spirit igniting the flame.

Each act of creation, a sacred embrace,
Transforming the ether, our own hidden place.
Together we forge what the eye cannot spy,
In sculpting the invisible, we learn to fly.

## The Art of Together

Two hands united, a tapestry bright,
Threads of our laughter, woven with light.
In every moment, a dance we create,
The rhythm of hearts, our unspoken fate.

Step by step, on this winding road,
Hand in hand, we lighten the load.
In the gaps of our silence, we find our song,
An art of together, where both belong.

Softly we share the weight of our dreams,
Building our futures, or so it seems.
Each glance a promise, each touch a start,
The masterpiece growing, two souls, one heart.

In storms we stand, with colors so bright,
The palette of trust, our beacon of light.
Crafting forever, with patience and grace,
The art of together, we gently embrace.

With struggles we strengthen, with joys we ignite,
A canvas of memories, vivid and bright.
Together we flourish, like flowers in sun,
In the art of together, we are always one.

# Unspoken Pages

Between the lines, a story unfolds,
In whispers of ink, our truth it holds.
Each unturned page, a mystery lies,
The depth of our thoughts, hidden from skies.

Ghosts of our voices, echo in dreams,
Silent confessions flow like clear streams.
Words left unspoken, yet loud and clear,
In the spaces where silence draws near.

Ink spills our secrets, on paper worn thin,
Tales of our battles, and where we've been.
With every unvoiced thought, a bridge we build,\nIn
unspoken pages, our hearts are filled.

The beauty of silence we both understand,
A language of souls, forever hand in hand.
As we turn each page, our stories entwine,
In the parchment of life, your heart next to mine.

We cherish the silence, the unsaid embrace,
The pages of life, a rhythmic chase.
In writing our truth, we silently rage,
Lost in the world of unspoken pages.

# Unraveled Secrets

In shadows of twilight, whispers conspire,
Tales of our secrets, sparked by the fire.
Unraveled threads of a life once concealed,\nIn the heart
of the chaos, our truth is revealed.

Beneath the facade, where shadows do play,
A dance of the hidden, night turns to day.
With every quiet moment, the past intertwines,
In the fabric of secrets, the future aligns.

Each glance a reminder, of stories so deep,
Guardians of treasures that we vow to keep.
With each shared silence, layers unfold,
Unraveled secrets, like raindrops turned gold.

We gather our stories, both bitter and sweet,
Embracing the power of vulnerability's beat.
In the warmth of your presence, our secrets unite,
In the whispers of trust, we find our light.

In the gentle twilight, our truths take flight,
Unraveling secrets, we conquer the night.
As woven together, our spirits set free,
In the tapestry of life, just you and me.

## Mosaic of Promise

In the quiet dawn of light,
Dreams begin to take their flight.
Colors blend in soft embrace,
Patterns weave in time and space.

Each piece a story to unfold,
Braving winds, both fierce and bold.
Shadows dance in vivid hues,
Cherishing both old and new.

Hope ignites in every heart,
Crafting beauty, every part.
Together, we will find our way,
In this mosaic of the day.

Hand in hand, we forge ahead,
With every tear and word unsaid.
The past behind, the future bright,
In unity, we claim our right.

A canvas rich with memories,
Each brushstroke whispers gentle pleas.
In this journey, we will thrive,
Mosaic of promise, alive.

## Echoing Heartbeats

In the stillness of the night,
Whispers echo, soft and light.
Two souls dancing, intertwined,
In rhythm, fate has aligned.

Every heartbeat tells a tale,
In the silence, love prevails.
Synchronized in breath and space,
Finding solace in embrace.

Time may test the bond we share,
Yet our vows will linger there.
Through the storms, we'll always stand,
Echoes of hearts, hand in hand.

Moments fade but love remains,
Infinite in all its chains.
In each thump, a promise kept,
Echoing where our spirits leapt.

Let the world drift far away,
In this rhythm, we shall sway.
For in every soft heartbeat,
Our love dances, pure and sweet.

## Tender Footprints

Along the shore, the waves retreat,
Leaving soft prints where we meet.
With every step, a story told,
A journey shared, a bond so bold.

Underneath the sunlit sky,
We chase the dreams that flutter by.
Hand in hand, we roam the land,
Building castles, grains of sand.

Footprints that the tides can't claim,
In our hearts, we'll stake our name.
Every path leads back to you,
In this dance of life, so true.

Seasons change, but love stays near,
In the laughter, in the cheer.
Through the storms and sunny days,
Tender footprints mark our ways.

So let us walk this path together,
Through the harsh and gentle weather.
With every footprint side by side,
We'll leave traces of our pride.

# Unveiling Layers

Beneath the surface, colors hide,
Layers deep, where dreams reside.
Peel away the masks we wear,
To find the truth, raw and rare.

In the quiet, whispers grow,
Secrets buried, tales to show.
As we delve into the deep,
Courage stirs where shadows creep.

Every layer tells a story,
Of pain, of growth, of fleeting glory.
With gentle hands, we must explore,
What lies beneath, we can restore.

Finding beauty in each crack,
In every journey's winding track.
As we shed what holds us back,
Unveiling layers, we stay on track.

So take my hand, let's seek the light,
Together, we will shine so bright.
In the layers, love reveals,
The essence of what truly heals.

# Chiaroscuro of Hearts

In shadows deep, where secrets sigh,
Two souls entwined, they dance and fly.
Light breaks forth, revealing fears,
Amidst the dark, love's truth appears.

Moments flicker, like candle's flame,
Whispers echo, calling their name.
In contrasts bold, their feelings flare,
A spectrum vast, both love and despair.

Soft glances shared, a gentle tease,
Hearts oscillate, like trembling leaves.
Each pulse a story, woven tight,
In chiaroscuro, love finds its light.

Through joy and pain, they carve their path,
In twilight's grasp, they learn to laugh.
The dance of light, the sway of dark,
Reveal the truth, ignite the spark.

So hand in hand, they walk the line,
In tender shades, their hearts align.
A canvas painted, rich and rare,
In chiaroscuro, love lays bare.

# Intimacy in Silence

In quiet corners, shadows blend,
Words unspoken, hearts extend.
Beneath the murmur, deep and wide,
Silent bonds, where truths abide.

Eyes that linger, softly glaze,
In every breath, a whispered praise.
Moments stretched, like golden threads,
In silence vast, our spirit spreads.

Hands that brush in gentle grace,
Time suspended, in this space.
No need for noise, just tender gaze,
In intimacy, our hearts ablaze.

With every heartbeat, a story spun,
In hushed tones, we become one.
Language lost, but feelings found,
In quietude, our love unbound.

So let the world fade to a hush,
In silence sweet, we find our rush.
With every pause, our souls ignite,
In intimacy, love takes flight.

## Veils of Understanding

Through layers thick, the truth unfolds,
In stories shared, and hands that hold.
A tapestry of night and day,
In veils of time, we find our way.

Where silence lingers, whispers wane,
Compassion blooms through joy and pain.
Each glance exchanged, a bridge we build,
In understanding, two hearts are thrilled.

Past wounds healed, with tender grace,
In gentle eyes, we find our place.
The fabric woven, rich and fine,
Through veils of life, our souls entwine.

And when the storm begins to roar,
In knowing glances, we find the core.
Together strong, we brave the tide,
In veils of understanding, side by side.

So let us dance through life's embrace,
With open hearts, and endless space.
Unraveling the layers seamed,
In veils of understanding, love redeemed.

# Brush of Serenity

With every stroke, a calm descends,
In gentle hues, the chaos ends.
Waves of stillness, brush the shore,
In serenity, we find our core.

Footprints traced on soft earth's face,
Laughter echoes, a warm embrace.
Nature whispers, as hearts align,
In peaceful moments, souls combine.

Clouds drift softly, like thoughts released,
In tranquil hours, our worries ceased.
A brush of colors, life's sweet art,
In serenity, we mend the heart.

So take my hand, let's wander free,
Through quiet woods and emerald sea.
In every breath, let stillness grow,
With brush of serenity, we go slow.

In whispers soft, the world unwinds,
In gentle peace, our love reminds.
Within our hearts, a calm decree,
With every brush, we find harmony.

# Fragments of Tenderness

In whispers soft and low,
We find the warmth of love's glow.
A touch, a glance, a fleeting breath,
In fragments, we dance through life and death.

The heart reveals its hidden seams,
Stitching together shattered dreams.
With every tear, a lesson learned,
In tenderness, our spirits burned.

We gather pieces from the past,
In moments fleeting, love holds fast.
A gentle word, a knowing smile,
Each fragment worth the aching mile.

In arms that cradle hope and fear,
We share our laughter, shed our tears.
A symphony of soft embrace,
In fragments found, we find our place.

Together, we'll mend what's torn,
Through tender nights and early morn.
With every beat, our hearts align,
In this sweet chaos, love's design.

# Palette of Secrets

A canvas brushed with muted hues,
Each color whispers hidden truths.
In shadows deep, the stories hide,
A palette rich, where dreams abide.

The azure blue of longing skies,
Emerald greens, where hope still lies.
Crimson red, the passion's fire,
In layers thick, we build our desire.

With every stroke, a secret spills,
A burst of joy, a hint of thrills.
In quiet corners, silence sings,
A dance of thoughts, of delicate things.

Golden yellows of warm embrace,
Soft pastels in a cherished space.
We mix and blend, we shape and mold,
In this artwork, our hearts unfold.

Each hue a moment, rich with light,
In every secret, day and night.
A masterpiece that time bestows,
Within this palette, love still grows.

## Captured in Silhouette

Beneath the moon's pale, gentle glow,
Figures dance in shadows low.
Silent whispers, secrets shared,
In silhouette, our spirits bared.

The outline of our fleeting dreams,
In twilight's grasp, nothing seems.
A silhouette against the night,
Capturing love in soft moonlight.

With hands entwined, we drift away,
In shadows cast, we dare to stay.
This fleeting moment, forever real,
Captured heartbeats, our love's appeal.

The world fades, and time stands still,
In silhouettes, we bend our will.
Against the dawn's brightening hue,
Our whispers turn to morning dew.

As day breaks, our shadows merge,
In light's embrace, we feel a surge.
Captured in silhouettes divine,
Your heart forever linked with mine.

# Beneath the Surface

The ocean sways with secrets deep,
In hidden depths where shadows sleep.
Beneath the waves, the whispers sigh,
A world alive where dreams can fly.

Coral dreams in vibrant hues,
Beneath the surface, life renews.
Gravity holds, yet freedom roams,
In watery realms, we find our homes.

The dance of fish, a fleeting glance,
In currents' sway, they twist and prance.
What lies unseen beneath the tide,
In depths unknown, our fears will hide.

A treasure trove of shimmering light,
In every bubble, pure delight.
Beneath the surface, we explore,
A hidden life, forevermore.

So dive with me, in oceans vast,
Let go of fears, embrace the cast.
Beneath the waves, we'll brave the cold,
In depths of love, our souls unfold.

## Tender Echoes

In the quiet of the night,
Whispers float like feathered light.
Heartbeats dance with soft despair,
Tender echoes linger everywhere.

Moonlight bathes the silent trees,
Caresses shadows with gentle ease.
Each sigh a reminder of love's embrace,
In tender echoes, we find our place.

Time stands still in gentle grace,
Memories etched on every face.
Fleeting moments, forever cherished,
In the heart's garden, they will not perish.

Stars above twinkle and gleam,
Reflecting all we dare to dream.
In the night, our souls entwine,
In tender echoes, love will shine.

## Anatomy of an Embrace

Fingers interlaced in trust,
Binding hearts, a sacred rust.
Every heartbeat, a silent song,
In this embrace, we both belong.

Breathless warmth in the cool night air,
A dance of souls, stripped of despair.
The curves and lines of bodies meet,
Anatomy of love, bittersweet.

Time suspends with every sigh,
Lost in the depths of each other's eye.
In the softness, we find our truth,
Echoes of wisdom, whispers of youth.

Moments flow like rivers wide,
In this embrace, we shall abide.
Every touch, a story to tell,
In the anatomy of love, we dwell.

# Harmony in Flesh

In a world that spins and breaks,
Our bodies dance for love's sweet stakes.
Skin on skin, a perfect blend,
Harmony in flesh, without end.

Notes of laughter fill the air,
Every glance, a precious flare.
In rhythm, our hearts unite,
In harmony, we bask in light.

Every heartbeat sings a song,
In this symphony, we belong.
Vibrations pulse in lingering grace,
A melody shared in this embrace.

Weaving feelings, threads of fire,
Binding dreams with hearts' desire.
In the dance of love, we confess,
In harmony of flesh, we find our bliss.

# Faded Memories on the Canvas

Brushstrokes whisper tales untold,
Of faded moments turned to gold.
Colors blend in twilight's glow,
On the canvas of hearts, love will flow.

Each hue a memory softly speaks,
In the silence, the heart still seeks.
Fingers trace where dreams had been,
Faded memories linger within.

Time erases but cannot sever,
The bonds we weave, a bond forever.
In every line, the laughter hums,
In faded memories, love becomes.

Dreams unfold in a gentle sway,
Painting shadows of yesterday.
In the canvas of time, we bloom,
Faded memories bring light from gloom.

# Savoring the Unseen

In shadows where whispers sway,
Secret moments softly play.
Gentle sighs beneath the stars,
Each touch a dance, a world of ours.

Fleeting glances, silent touches,
In heartbeats, love constructs.
The magic in the still of night,
Brings hidden dreams into the light.

In the rustle of the leaves,
Life is more than it perceives.
Each heartbeat holds a tender grace,
A treasure in this quiet space.

Taste the silence, feel the air,
Moments linger everywhere.
Between the lines, life unfolds,
In bittersweet, the truth beholds.

So let us savor, gentle, dear,
The unseen paths that brought us here.
In each breath, we find our way,
Together, always, night and day.

# The Essence of Us

In twilight's glow, our shadows merge,
Two souls alight, a gentle surge.
Within the laughter, we ignite,
A bond that shines, pure and bright.

Threads of trust weave through the night,
Connecting dreams, a shared flight.
In every heartbeat, stories blend,
The essence of us, without end.

With each sunrise, we arise anew,
In shared moments, the world feels true.
Hands entwined, the journey flows,
In every pulse, our love bestows.

Through whispered words and soft embrace,
We find our rhythm, our special place.
In the dance of life, we lose control,
Yet find the essence of every soul.

So let us cherish, day by day,
The love we nurture and the way.
Together, through the storms, we trust,
In the essence of us, we must.

# Harmonies Shared

In the quiet of the morning light,
Harmonies rise, taking flight.
Notes of laughter fill the air,
A melody only we can share.

Each moment sings a different tune,
Underneath the watching moon.
Together we dance, lost in the sound,
In harmonies shared, love is found.

With every breath, we craft our song,
In the world where we both belong.
The rhythm of hearts, the softest beat,
A symphony where souls meet.

In the whispers of the evening breeze,
Our hearts compose, aiming to please.
Defined by love, our voices blend,
In harmony shared, there's no end.

So let the music play on bright,
In every shadow and every light.
Together, we'll write our refrain,
In harmonies shared, joy will remain.

# Glimmers of Togetherness

In the canvas of stars, we find,
Glimmers of dreams artfully aligned.
Each sparkle tells a tale untold,
In the silence, our love unfolds.

Through every trial, side by side,
In the depths, we learn to glide.
Together, building castles high,
With glimpses of joy that touch the sky.

In laughter and tears, we hold dear,
Moments that bring us close and near.
In every heartbeat, time stands still,
Glimmers of us, a perfect thrill.

As seasons change and time flows on,
In warm embraces, we've grown strong.
These glimmers of joy, a gentle kiss,
Remind us why we chose this bliss.

So let us treasure what we share,
In every whisper, every prayer.
With glimmers of togetherness bright,
We find our path in love's soft light.

# Close Enough to Breathe

In the silence where shadows play,
Our whispers linger, soft as clay.
Hands almost touching, hearts in tune,
Under the watch of a crescent moon.

The space between feels warm, yet chill,
A dance of souls, an unspoken thrill.
With every glance, we draw the line,
Close enough to breathe, but not to bind.

Stars above mirror our sighs,
Reflecting dreams in quiet skies.
We chase the night, a fleeting chance,
In the darkness, we find our dance.

Every heartbeat echoes a song,
In this moment where we belong.
Fingers brush in a tangled weave,
Close enough to breathe, we believe.

In fleeting time, we hesitate,
The pull of fate, we contemplate.
With every beat, we edge so near,
Close enough to breathe, yet unclear.

# The Geometry of Us

In distant corners and foreshadowed lines,
We trace the shapes where our heart aligns.
Angles sharp, yet softly meet,
In the geometry of love, so sweet.

Circles spin with a gentle grace,
In your laughter, I find my place.
A perfect square, we stand so strong,
In this tapestry, where we belong.

The curves of fate chart our course,
Guiding us through with unseen force.
Vectors pull in a cosmic dance,
Mathematics of love, a timeless chance.

As parallel lines, we search the skies,
In a world of tangents, our spirits rise.
Each intersection, a moment spent,
The geometry of us, heaven-sent.

With every shape, we redefine,
A masterpiece in perfect time.
In every heartbeat, a truth we trust,
Forever bound in the geometry of us.

## Unspoken Bonds

In the quiet spaces where shadows hide,
A bond unbroken, time as our guide.
Eyes that speak when words fall short,
In unspoken bonds, our hearts resort.

We share a world of secret thoughts,
In the silence, love never rots.
Through storms and trials, we stand as one,
Every sunset whispers, we're never done.

Threads of fate weave our connection,
Invisible ties without direction.
In gentle gestures, warmth we find,
Unspoken bonds, eternally aligned.

In crowded rooms, we know the tune,
Dancing lost beneath the moon.
In laughter shared and silent tears,
A world of love, beyond the years.

So here we stand, without a plea,
In unspoken bonds, just you and me.
Our hearts compose a timeless song,
An echo of us, forever strong.

# Fusions of Soul

In the depths where shadows roam,
We find the light, we call it home.
Fusions of soul, a spark divine,
In the merging of hearts, a sacred sign.

With every glance, a universe sparks,
In the silence, we leave our marks.
Together we pulse, a single beat,
In fusions of soul, we are complete.

The colors dance in vibrant hues,
Painting dreams in twilight views.
With every breath, we intertwine,
In this tapestry, we shine.

In the rhythm of waves, we stand tall,
Together we rise, never to fall.
In the depths of night, we find our grace,
Fusions of soul, a warm embrace.

So let us journey, hand in hand,
Through all the wonders, we take our stand.
In love's embrace, we become whole,
In fusions of our intertwining soul.

# Tides of Intimacy

The waves roll softly to the shore,
Whispers of secrets we both adore.
In the ebb, our hearts find their way,
Crashing tides of love in delicate sway.

Moonlight dances on the sea's embrace,
Holding you close in this sacred space.
With each surge, our souls intertwine,
In the ocean's depth, you're truly mine.

The currents pull, then gently release,
In our embrace, we discover peace.
Together we float, forever we glide,
On this voyage, we're side by side.

Footprints in sand, washed away by time,
Yet the spirit remains, forever to climb.
With each new wave, our love does grow,
In the rhythm of tides, our spirits flow.

As the sun sets, painting skies in gold,
Our hearts beat as one, stories unfold.
Each tide that moves, a gentle caress,
In this ocean of love, we are blessed.

# Journeys in Each Other's Eyes

Every glance leads us to new heights,
A universe spun in tender sights.
With a look, we travel vast lands,
Exploring dreams with intertwined hands.

Your spark ignites a passionate fire,
In your gaze, I find my desire.
Windows to souls, so deep, so true,
Journeys await, just me and you.

Through stormy clouds and sunny days,
In each glance, our love always stays.
Silent conversations, profound and wise,
Holding galaxies in each other's eyes.

We write stories, verse by verse,
In every look, no need to rehearse.
The world fades away, just us two,
Within this journey, I see you.

With every blink, memories recast,
Reflecting future and honoring past.
In the depths of love, where time lies still,
Our eyes meet, and the world feels fulfilled.

## Echoes of Affection

In whispers soft, affection sings,
Gentle echoes of tender things.
In every heartbeat, a rhythm flows,
Love's melody, a sweet repose.

The warmth of your touch, an embrace divine,
In moments shared, our hearts align.
With every laugh, echoes resonate,
A symphony of love we create.

Memories linger, vivid and bright,
Painting our world, a beautiful sight.
In the silence, our souls communicate,
A bond so strong, it never abates.

The stars conspire in the night sky's scheme,
Reflecting our love, a shared dream.
With every glance, the echoes remain,
In this dance of affection, there's no pain.

Together we rise, with the dawn's first light,
In the echoes of love, everything feels right.
With every word, we weave our song,
In this embrace, we forever belong.

# Frames of Emotion

In every photo, a moment caught,
A frame of emotion, love's perfect thought.
Captured smiles and laughter bright,
In these memories, our hearts ignite.

The stories told in shadows and light,
Each image speaks of pure delight.
In these frames, our souls align,
A gallery where love intertwines.

Every glance recalls the warmth we know,
Through these pictures, our spirits glow.
In every snapshot, time stands still,
A testament to love's endless thrill.

With each frame, our love's tale grows,
In colors vibrant, as the heart bestows.
Moments frozen, yet alive with grace,
In this world, we find our place.

As the years pass, our collection expands,
A tapestry woven with loving hands.
In frames of emotion, we will reside,
Together forever, our hearts open wide.

# Strokes of Affection

In every gentle touch, a feeling,
A soft whisper shared, revealing.
Brush of hands, a warm embrace,
Hearts entwined in sacred space.

The color glows in twilight's hue,
With every glance, a love so true.
Each smile a canvas, bright and bold,
A tapestry of stories told.

In laughter's echo, dreams take flight,
With every heartbeat, pure delight.
Gentle strokes of fate align,
In love's sweet dance, we intertwine.

Under skies of stars, we sway,
Guided by hope's soft ballet.
As shadows blend and daylight fades,
Our bond remains, the heart's cascades.

In quiet moments, joy's refrain,
A timeless song that soothes the pain.
With every step, we leave a mark,
In love's embrace, we spark the dark.

# Murmurs in Color

Whispers of wind through emerald trees,
Brush of twilight on soft seas.
In the silence, colors merge,
From dreams, a vibrant urge.

Golden rays of sun's embrace,
Painting shadows on your face.
Every hue tells a tale,
Of love that will never pale.

The deep blue of an endless sky,
Echoes of the lark's sweet cry.
In petals' dance, life unfolds,
Murmurs of love, soft and bold.

In twilight's blush, secrets bloom,
In every space, a gentle room.
Where laughter fills the air with cheer,
And every note, a song so clear.

As night descends with velvet grace,
Stars gather, our hearts' embrace.
In every color, a lifeline drawn,
Murmurs of love greet the dawn.

# Caress of the Muse

In whispers soft, art finds its flight,
Where shadows blend with morning light.
The muse dances on inspired dreams,
In vivid hues, the heart redeems.

With every brushstroke, feelings arise,
Unveiling worlds with sparkling eyes.
In silence lingers a sweet refrain,
A melody born from joy and pain.

Through tangled thoughts, creation flows,
Imagination, where passion grows.
With rhythm, the soul begins to sing,
Awakening magic in everything.

In fleeting moments, life takes shape,
Through vibrant colors, we escape.
The muse's touch, a tender guide,
Unfolding dreams, we cannot hide.

As twilight whispers, stories gleam,
In love's embrace, we find our theme.
With every sigh, the world we choose,
In the caress of the muse, we lose.

# Embrace of Shadows

In the quiet dusk, shadows weave,
A gentle touch that helps us grieve.
In soft murmurs, secrets hide,
The night unfolds, a comforting guide.

Dusky hues wrapped in mystery,
Woven in threads of history.
As stars appear, the heart's delight,
In shadows, we find our light.

Each sigh a story left unsaid,
In the moon's glow, fears are shed.
Embracing darkness, we take flight,
With hopes alight, as dreams ignite.

Through silence deep, the whispers call,
In shadows cast, we stand tall.
With every heartbeat, close we tread,
In love's embrace, we forge ahead.

In the fading light, shadows dance,
A tender waltz, a sacred chance.
With every moment, together we grow,
In the embrace of shadows, we glow.

## Silent Conversations

In whispers soft, the silence grows,
Words unspoken, a world in prose.
Thoughts entwined in shadows deep,
Promises made that we must keep.

Glimmers of hope in the quiet night,
Hearts beat gently, hidden from sight.
Echoes linger where dreams reside,
Silent vows cannot hide.

With every glance, a story unfolds,
In the stillness, more than words told.
Hands brush lightly, a fleeting touch,
In this silence, we feel so much.

Time stands still in moments rare,
A connection felt in the open air.
In the quiet, we find our way,
Silent conversations lead us to stay.

As night deepens, stars align,
Two souls lost in a perfect design.
In every pause, a promise made,
In the silence, love won't fade.

## Threads of Soul

Like threads that weave through life's great loom,
Connecting paths, dispelling gloom.
Each color bright, a story spun,
A tapestry of souls as one.

In every twist, a lesson learned,
In every knot, a passion burned.
Silent bonds that time can't sever,
Threads of soul, forever and ever.

With gentle hands, we craft our fate,
Each moment cherished, never late.
Strong and fragile, we intertwine,
In the fabric of life, you are mine.

As seasons change, our threads will blend,
Through storms and sun, we will transcend.
A vibrant dance, this life we share,
In every heartbeat, we find care.

Together woven, we rise and fall,
In this grand design, we embrace it all.
With every stitch, our journeys told,
Threads of soul, pure as gold.

# Canvas of Emotions

Upon a canvas, colors collide,
Each stroke a feeling we cannot hide.
Blues of sorrow, reds of bliss,
In this art, we find our kiss.

With every hue, our stories unfold,
Brushes dance as memories hold.
Whispers of joy in golden light,
Creating glimpses of pure delight.

In shadows cast, the heart reveals,
The depth of love, the pain it heals.
A masterpiece born from tears and laughter,
In every corner, forever after.

As seasons shift the palette's frame,
Each moment captured, never the same.
In vibrant strokes, our truth is shown,
A canvas of emotions, never alone.

With every glance, we're drawn to see,
The beauty of life's intricate tapestry.
In this artwork, our spirits soar,
Canvas of emotions, forevermore.

# Dancing Shadows of Love

In the twilight, shadows play,
Two souls embrace at the end of day.
Softly whispered secrets exchanged,
Dancing shadows, sweet and strange.

Underneath the fading light,
Hearts entwined, everything feels right.
With every step, we lose control,
In this dance, we find our soul.

Moonlight glimmers on the ground,
In the silence, our love is found.
Twisting, turning, lost in the night,
In dancing shadows, we find our light.

With gentle hands, we hold on tight,
In this moment, pure and bright.
Every glance, a promise made,
In the depths of love, we won't fade.

As dawn approaches, the shadows wane,
But our dance will always remain.
In every heartbeat, our spirits sway,
Dancing shadows, come what may.

## Fragments of Us

In shadows cast by whispered time,
We piece together what's been lost.
Each memory a fragile rhyme,
A tapestry we've slowly crossed.

Scattered dreams on windswept nights,
Fragments glinting in the dark.
We search for joy in fleeting sights,
The echo of a hopeful spark.

Once vibrant hearts in silent sighs,
Rekindled by the warmth of touch.
In every gaze, the love still flies,
The bond that holds us, fierce and such.

We gather pieces, paint our souls,
Brushing edges of our pain.
With every pulse, the story rolls,
Like falling leaves in autumn's rain.

A constellation forged by tears,
We find the light in storms above.
For in the fragments of our years,
We learn the art of holding love.

# Chasing Vulnerability

In the quiet, hearts lay bare,
Fearing storms yet yearning still.
With every truth, we bravely dare,
To dive into the gentle chill.

Words unspoken, secrets shared,
Navigating paths of doubt.
Knowing that we are ensnared,
By the love that's born from routes.

With open arms, we reach and fall,
Creating bridges, daring flight.
In each embrace, we hear the call,
Chasing shadows, embracing light.

Beneath the skin, where feelings weave,
We find the echoes of our truth.
In vulnerability, we believe,
A dance of trust, a timeless youth.

For when we meet our tender fears,
We learn the strength of honest hearts.
In these moments, through our tears,
We rise anew as love imparts.

**Sculpting Moments**


With tender hands, we mold our days,
Chiseling time from marble grey.
Every giggle, every praise,
Crafting joy in our own way.

In the laughter, memories form,
Like clay beneath our fingertips.
We shape the calm, embrace the storm,
Creating stories that eclipse.

Each fleeting glance a masterpiece,
A fleeting touch becomes so grand.
In every heartbeat, sweet release,
We sketch our lives, hand in hand.

Fragments of now, forever cast,
In the gallery of our years.
A sculptor's love, both bold and vast,
Transforming whispers into cheers.

In stillness found in fleeting breath,
We carve our names in silken air.
A blend of life, a dance with death,
Sculpting moments we both share.

# The Language of Closeness

In silence, words often spill,
Across the gap, a thread we weave.
With every glance, our spirits thrill,
A connection that we both believe.

The rhythm found in heartbeats' flow,
Translates the distance into song.
In gestures soft, we come to know,
Life's melody, where we belong.

Unspoken vows in every sigh,
A symphony of breath and space.
We speak in brushed hands, you and I,
The language of our warm embrace.

With laughter's spark and tenderness,
We build the bridge that brings us near.
In shared dreams, we're free to press,
The whispering truth that we both hear.

Each moment spent, a tale unfolds,
In gestures clear, we find our tone.
In closeness, love forever holds,
A sacred bond, a heart's true home.

# Murmurs in the Dark

In silence we wander, shadows embrace,
Whispers of dreams in a secret place.
Stars above glimmer, soft and bright,
Veils of the night hide our delight.

Ghosts of the past, they softly call,
Echoes of laughter, we rise and fall.
Heartbeats in rhythm, a soft refrain,
Minds intertwined in pleasure and pain.

Lost in the stillness where shadows play,
Time stands suspended, night turns to day.
Under the moonlight, courage we find,
Murmurs of love in the depths of the mind.

Breath of the evening, cool on our skin,
Promises spoken, where all begins.
In the embrace of the twilight's hand,
Whispers of secrets in darkened land.

In the heart's chamber, where dreams ignite,
Murmurs like music dance through the night.
Together we linger, forever we stay,
In the sweet silence, love finds its way.

# Palette of Secrets

Brush strokes of mystery, colors in flight,
Canvas of whispers, hidden from sight.
Each hue a tale of love and of pain,
Palette of secrets, bliss mixed with rain.

Crimson for passion, and azure for calm,
Every layer crafted, a delicate balm.
Emerald dreams, they shimmer and gleam,
A portrait of stories, stitched with a seam.

Golden horizons where laughter was spun,
Canvas of memories, moments undone.
Shadows that linger in twilight's warm glow,
Palette of wishes, the heart's undertow.

Splashes of silence, the ink of the night,
Every drop radiant, vivid with light.
We paint our journey through colors so bold,
Palette of whispers, rich tales to be told.

Guided by dreams, we sketch our desires,
Creating a world that never expires.
In this rich tapestry, our spirits take flight,
Palette of secrets, we dance in the light.

## Kisses in the Shadows

In the dusk of twilight, softly we meet,
A brush of your lips, so tender and sweet.
Caught in the moment, the world fades away,
Kisses in shadows, where hearts come to play.

Flickers of laughter, a spark in the air,
Whispers of longing, both humble and rare.
The night wraps around us, a warm velvet cloak,
Kisses like secrets, unspoken yet woke.

Beneath the stars, where time drifts apart,
Every stolen glance, a song from the heart.
In this quiet chaos, we lose and we find,
Kisses in shadows, our souls intertwined.

Moments like petals, they slip through our hold,
Stories of yearning, in silence retold.
With every soft touch, the darkness ignites,
Kisses like stardust in velvety nights.

Embracing the stillness, we breathe in the night,
Kisses in shadows, a muse to our flight.
Hand in hand we wander, through echoes and dreams,
In whispers of twilight, love flows in streams.

# Fingers Entwined

Under the starlight, we find our way,
Fingers entwined, come what may.
Softly we wander, hearts intertwined,
In this sacred moment, pure love defined.

The world fades away, just you and I,
Bound by the starlight, reaching the sky.
Each touch a promise, each glance a sign,
Two souls as one, with fingers entwined.

Echoes of laughter, a sweet melody,
In the dance of the night, we're wild and free.
Every heartbeat whispers a tale so divine,
In the hush of the twilight, fingers entwined.

Time drifts like petals in the softest breeze,
Wrapped in this moment, we do as we please.
With dreams held close, we gently align,
In shadows of silence, our fingers entwined.

Through ups and downs, we'll weather the storm,
Together we rise, in each other we're warm.
In the story of us, love is the line,
Written forever with fingers entwined.

# In the Quiet Hours

Whispers of the night wrap me tight,
Stars flicker softly, shining bright.
Moments linger, time stands still,
In solitude, my heart does fill.

Shadows dance, a gentle sway,
Candle flames flicker, guiding the way.
Thoughts drift softly, like a breeze,
In the stillness, my soul finds ease.

The world outside fades away,
Here in silence, I choose to stay.
Each breath a note, a quiet song,
In these hours, where I belong.

Memories whisper, tales unfold,
In the quiet, secrets told.
Time stands still in twilight's glow,
In the quiet hours, peace does flow.

Embracing the calm, wrapped in the night,
Finding comfort in the soft moonlight.
With each heartbeat, I become aware,
In the silence, I'm free, laid bare.

# The Dance of Two

In the moonlight, we find our spark,
Two souls entwined, lighting the dark.
With every step, a rhythm divine,
We sway as one, your heart with mine.

The music swells, lifting us high,
In each other's gaze, we touch the sky.
Together we twirl, lost in the night,
In this dance, everything feels right.

Hands clasped tight, a promise made,
In this fleeting moment, fears do fade.
With every turn, the world disappears,
Only the music, your whispers near.

The stars applaud our graceful flight,
In this dance, we ignite the night.
Two hearts beating, a timeless embrace,
With every step, we find our place.

As the last note lingers on,
In this dance, our love is drawn.
With tired feet but spirits so free,
Together we dance, just you and me.

## Messages Between Breaths

In the pause between heartbeats,
Words unspoken, a truth that greets.
Glimmers of thought in silence arise,
In stillness, our souls intertwine.

Just a sigh, and the world will see,
Every whisper, a part of me.
In the quiet, where feelings blend,
Messages shared that never end.

Breaths like petals, soft and light,
Each inhale, a dream in flight.
Emotions dance on the edge of sound,
In this space, our hearts are found.

With every pause, a deeper truth,
In silence, we reclaim our youth.
Thoughts take shape, weaving through,
Messages spoken in shades of blue.

The rhythm of life, gentle and clear,
In each breath, I hold you near.
Moments crafted in quiet grace,
Messages shared in this sacred space.

# Chasing the Dusk

As the sun dips low, colors ignite,
Day bids farewell, embracing the night.
With every hue, a story to tell,
In twilight's arms, all is well.

Shadows stretch, the world transforms,
In the gentle breeze, my spirit warms.
Chasing the dusk, where dreams begin,
In the stillness, I let you in.

Stars awaken, one by one,
Winking at secrets, the day is done.
With each breath, I feel the pull,
Chasing the dusk, my heart is full.

Moonlight spills, a silver stream,
Guiding the way, like a soft dream.
In the quiet of night, I feel so free,
Chasing the dusk, it's you and me.

Tomorrow awaits, but for now, we play,
In dusk's embrace, we drift away.
With every moment, the magic grows,
Chasing the dusk, where love flows.

## In the Embrace of Understanding

In shadows cast by gentle light,
Two hearts converge, a soft ignite.
Whispers dance in the quiet air,
Bound by threads of tender care.

Time stands still in this sacred space,
Eyes reflect a familiar grace.
Every sigh wrapped in trust,
Building dreams from the dust.

Silent promises spoken loud,
In this moment, hearts are proud.
Understanding flows like a stream,
Merging hopes into one dream.

Through storms that threaten to sway,
Together they find a way.
With hands entwined, they will rise,
Finding strength in shared skies.

In each embrace, a new dawn breaks,
Love like water in gentle lakes.
This journey is theirs to pave,
In the embrace of brave hearts so brave.

# Ceremony of Souls

In twilight's glow, spirits align,
Whispers echo through the pine.
Candles flicker, a guiding light,
Inviting souls to join the night.

Rituals soar on the breath of wind,
Stories of loss and love rescind.
Chants rise like an ancient song,
In this place where they belong.

Gaze into the sacred fire,
Witness flames that never tire.
Each ember holds a dream once shared,
A testament of lives declared.

As stars adorn the velvet sky,
Memories dance, they never die.
With every heartbeat, a promise made,
In unity, never to fade.

The circle formed, hands intertwine,
In this ceremony, souls combine.
Together they weave a tapestry,
A legacy of eternity.

# Woven Whispers

In the quiet of the morning dew,
Whispers of the day break through.
Threads of light across the grass,
Nature's secrets come to pass.

Each breeze carries tales anew,
Of dreams chased and hopes pursued.
In the melody of a soft song,
Woven whispers where we belong.

Underneath the sprawling trees,
Stories flow like gentle streams.
Leaves rustle with the softest sigh,
Reminding us of the why.

The sun dips low, a vibrant hue,
Painting skies in shades so true.
In this moment, hearts connect,
Woven whispers, deep respect.

As twilight descends, shadows blend,
We find solace, around the bend.
In every listen, a piece of art,
Woven whispers, heart to heart.

# Ripples of Trust

In still waters, reflections blend,
With every drop, we start to mend.
Secrets shared in hushed tones,
Creating ties that feel like homes.

A gentle touch, a knowing glance,
In ripples formed, a quiet dance.
Trust is built with every wave,
In the depths, it learns to brave.

Like the moon that pulls the tides,
In this bond, love never hides.
With every echo, hearts align,
Crafting stories, intertwine.

Through storms that test our very core,
Each ripple grows, a lasting shore.
Together we weather the unseen,
Ripples of trust, evergreen.

As seasons change and time flows free,
Our journey writes its mystery.
In the stillness, we hear the call,
Ripples of trust, connecting all.

# Crescendo of Longing

In quiet rooms, whispers swell,
Memories dance, a distant bell.
Fingers trace the air so thin,
A longing song begins to spin.

Each heartbeat echoes through the night,
A melody of wrong and right.
In shadows where the yearning thrives,
Euphoria in dreams survives.

With every rise, every fall,
The silence breathes, it knows it all.
A symphony of hopes untold,
In whispers soft, our hearts behold.

Through every tear, a note is played,
In twilight's glow, the music swayed.
In tangled thoughts, we find our way,
A crescendo of longing holds sway.

As sunrise breaks the night apart,
A quiet truth ignites the heart.
In every note that aches to be,
We find the power to be free.

## Waves of Surrender

The ocean breathes a gentle sigh,
In rhythm with the endless sky.
Each wave that crashes at my feet,
Calls me to dance, to feel complete.

With every ebb, a story fades,
In sinking sands, a memory wades.
The pull of tides, the moon's embrace,
In surrender lies a sacred space.

Drifting thoughts like seafoam swirl,
Wrapped in currents, I softly twirl.
The salt upon my lips, a kiss,
Reminds me of the ocean's bliss.

Beneath the starlit canopy,
All troubles drown, I am set free.
In the calm, I find my truth,
In waves of love, I stay uncouth.

With each retreat, I learn to crave,
The power in the quiet wave.
For in each surge, there lies the key,
To surrender to the vast, to be.

## Heartstrings in Harmony

A gentle strum on strings of gold,
Our stories whispered, love retold.
In perfect rhythm, hearts align,
Creating music, pure divine.

With every note, a bond is cast,
Each melody connects the past.
In laughter's echo, we find grace,
United in this sacred space.

Through joyful peaks and valleys low,
The heartstrings hum, they ebb and flow.
In symphony, we rise, we fall,
A tapestry, we weave it all.

With eyes closed tight, we dream awake,
In harmony, we learn to break.
Each whispered word, a tender touch,
In love's embrace, we feel so much.

The final chord fades into night,
Yet in our hearts, we hold the light.
A song remains, forever true,
In heartstrings' dance, we start anew.

# The Brush of Being

With colors bright, the canvas breathes,
Each stroke a story, life believes.
In hues of joy, in shades of pain,
A masterpiece from sun and rain.

The brush in hand, I seek to find,
The whispers woven in my mind.
Each flick, each smear, each gentle line,
In chaos, order, love divine.

The quiet splash of ocean's blue,
Invokes a dance, a spirit true.
From darkest nights to brightest dawn,
In every shade, my soul is drawn.

With every layer, I redefine,
The essence pure, the heart, the spine.
In strokes of wonder, shadows fade,
A world alive, a life portrayed.

As moments blend and colors merge,
I find my place, begin to surge.
With every breath, with every dream,
The brush of being moves like steam.

# Echoes in the Frame

Whispers of a time once known,
Captured in a glance,
Memories softly moan,
Fleeting in their dance.

Colors fade yet still remain,
Framed inside these walls,
Echoes of joy, echoes of pain,
In silence, the heart calls.

Each image tells a tale,
Of laughter, love, and fear,
A timeless, fragile veil,
Held close, yet far from here.

Reflections in the glass,
Glimmers of days gone by,
Moments that never pass,
They linger, they sigh.

Within this sacred space,
Past and present align,
Each face, a warm embrace,
In echoes, we find time.

# Portrait of a Moment

Brushstrokes of light and shade,
A smile caught in the air,
Where memories are laid,
And colors blend with care.

Candid glances hold the truth,
In stillness, we reflect,
The innocence of youth,
In time's gentle respect.

Fleeting chances we adore,
Captured in a frame,
Each glance reveals the core,
And whispers our names.

In shadows, laughter rings,
A heartbeat on display,
In every brush, it sings,
Of dreams that shape today.

A moment now defined,
In hues of love and grace,
The essence intertwined,
In this sacred space.

# In the Space Between

A pause in time we feel,
Where silence speaks so loud,
The unspoken is real,
A mystery avowed.

Invisible threads we weave,
Connecting heart to heart,
In moments we believe,
Is where we play our part.

Between the words we share,
A sacred bond takes flight,
In glances, in the air,
The day turns into night.

What lies beyond the veil,
In shadows soft and bright,
A delicate detail,
That dances in the light.

In the quiet we find peace,
A space, a shared embrace,
Where love will never cease,
In this enchanting place.

# Tapestry of Emotions

Threads of joy and sorrow,
Woven deep within the heart,
Each stitch a new tomorrow,
In life's intricate art.

Colors vibrant, pale, and bold,
A range of every hue,
Stories waiting to be told,
In fabric old and new.

Every tear and every grin,
Embroidery of the soul,
Show the battles deep within,
That makes the spirit whole.

We loom our fears and dreams,
A masterpiece on show,
In sunlight, shadows gleam,
In threads that ebb and flow.

A tapestry unraveled,
Where emotions intertwine,
In every piece, we traveled,
A story so divine.

# Mosaics of Affection

In every glance, a story told,
Fragments of warmth, a heart to hold.
Colors blend in soft embrace,
A tapestry woven, a sacred space.

Laughter dances like light on skin,
In quiet corners, love can begin.
Each smile a piece of shining glass,
Reflecting moments, as they pass.

Hands entwined, paths intertwined,
In the mosaic, connection defined.
Every crack, a chance to mend,
In this art, we find our blend.

Echoes of love in every hue,
Painting life with shades so true.
In this canvas, hearts reveal,
The beauty of how we feel.

Through time's passage, the pieces grow,
In the gallery of hearts, we glow.
The art of affection, a timeless quest,
In every mosaic, we are blessed.

## Symphony of Close Encounters

In the stillness, a note of grace,
Voices blend in this sacred space.
Strangers meet, hearts start to sway,
A melody forms, guiding the way.

Each heartbeat echoes, a rhythmic song,
Together we dance, where we belong.
In whispered tones, a sweet refrain,
The symphony swells, soothing our pain.

With every glance, a chord is struck,
In the harmony, we find our luck.
Melodies rise like stars in the night,
Close encounters, a wondrous sight.

Notes intertwine, like hands that meet,
This symphony, a sound so sweet.
Caught in a moment, time stands still,
In the music of us, we feel the thrill.

As daylight fades, the concert grows,
In the silence, our connection flows.
The symphony lingers, soft and clear,
In every heartbeat, I hold you near.

# Whispers of Connection

In the quiet, a soft voice calls,
A gentle whisper, where affection falls.
Eyes meet shyly, a spark ignites,
In unspoken words, our truth ignites.

Each shared glance holds a story new,
In the silence, I'm drawn to you.
The air is thick with dreams unsaid,
In whispered breaths, our hearts are led.

We weave a bond that few can see,
In the stillness, you're part of me.
Connections form like shadows cast,
In fleeting moments, we hold fast.

The world fades beneath this soft glow,
In whispers, our secrets start to flow.
A language of trust, tender and true,
In the quiet, I find you.

With each heartbeat, whispers grow bold,
In this sanctuary, we behold.
The threads of connection, woven tight,
In whispers of love, we find our light.

# Brushstrokes of Affection

In the canvas of our lives, we paint,
Each brushstroke whispers, soft and faint.
Colors blend in an endless swirl,
A masterpiece born as hearts unfurl.

With every touch, a hue is laid,
In the art of us, nothing's frayed.
An abstract dance, where feelings flow,
In brushstrokes of love, we gently grow.

Tints of laughter fill the air,
Creating scenes we're meant to share.
In every stroke, a memory shines,
A gallery of hearts, where love aligns.

Shadows deepen, highlights glow,
In each layer, our feelings show.
A palette rich with passions bright,
In the brush of affection, we find light.

As we paint this journey, side by side,
In the art of connection, we take pride.
Every canvas tells a story true,
In brushstrokes of love, I cherish you.

# Fleeting Sanctuaries

In the hush of twilight glow,
Whispers of dreams begin to flow.
Beneath the boughs where shadows dance,
We find our hearts in a fleeting trance.

Moments gathered like autumn leaves,
Each one cradled, as time deceives.
The echoes of laughter softly fade,
Leaving traces of joy that won't evade.

A sanctuary in each gentle breeze,
Where worries vanish with such ease.
Here, the world feels light and free,
In these spaces, just you and me.

Stars begin to inhabit the night,
Our burdens lifted, spirits in flight.
Each heartbeat syncs with the moon's embrace,
In fleeting sanctuaries, we find our place.

## In the Realm of You


In the soft glow of morning light,
Your laughter dances, pure delight.
Every glance, a secret shared,
In the realm of you, I am bared.

Time slows down, the world stands still,
Awash in moments, a timeless thrill.
With every heartbeat under the sky,
In the realm of you, I can't deny.

Your voice, a melody, sweet and clear,
Whispers of love that only I hear.
Every word, a soothing balm,
In the realm of you, I am calm.

Infinite paths where our fates entwine,
Each step forward, your hand in mine.
Lost in the wonders this world can do,
Forever anchored in the realm of you.

## Resonating Rhythms

Within each heartbeat, a rhythm's play,
A symphony crafted by night and day.
In movements gentle, the world aligns,
Resonating rhythms, hearts entwined.

The pulse of earth beneath our feet,
In perfect harmony, we find our beat.
Each note, a story, a tale to tell,
Resonating rhythms, casting a spell.

In shadows cast by the setting sun,
We dance together, two souls as one.
Every whisper a melodious tune,
In resonating rhythms, we find our moon.

Let the music guide us through the night,
Every step taken feels so right.
With every heartbeat, love's refrain,
In resonating rhythms, we'll remain.

## Gaze of Serenity

With a gaze that calms the storm inside,
In your eyes, the world can confide.
Each look a promise, soft and clear,
A gaze of serenity, drawing near.

The chaos fades in your gentle light,
As we navigate the calming night.
In silence spoken, our spirits soar,
In a gaze of serenity, we explore.

Beneath the stars, our worries cease,
In your presence, I find my peace.
Every heartbeat whispers "stay,"
In the gaze of serenity, come what may.

Time drifts softly, like clouds above,
Wrapped in comfort, wrapped in love.
Together we find, in the stillness, bliss,
In a gaze of serenity, a perfect kiss.

# Whispers of Canvas

In shadows soft, the colors blend,
A tale unfolds, where dreams ascend.
The silence speaks, in hues so bright,
Each stroke a sigh, a gentle light.

A whisper here, a shade of fate,
With each fine line, we contemplate.
The brush obeys, in dance so pure,
A silent bond, that will endure.

A canvas waits, with secrets deep,
In vibrant strokes, our hearts will leap.
As echoes paint, the love we share,
A masterpiece, beyond compare.

In every glance, a story told,
With every shade, our spirits bold.
We linger long, where colors meet,
And in that space, our souls repeat.

Together we, the artists dream,
In whispers soft, a flowing stream.
As colors merge, and life unfolds,
Our canvas bright, where love beholds.

## Brushstrokes of Connection

With every stroke, a bond is formed,
In colors bright, our hearts are warmed.
Awash in light, we find our way,
Through swirling hues, we dance and sway.

Each brush we use, a story shared,
In vibrant lines, we're truly bared.
From deep within, our spirits flow,
In every touch, the love we know.

United here, in strokes of grace,
We paint our dreams, we find our place.
The canvas wide, our hearts laid bare,
In every shade, we help each other care.

As colors mix, new worlds arise,
A tapestry that never lies.
In every hue, a truth revealed,
Through brushstrokes bold, our fate is sealed.

Together now, let's paint the night,
In shared delight, with hearts alight.
With every stroke, our spirits sing,
Brushstrokes of love, forever cling.

# In the Silken Glow

In twilight's hush, the glimmer grows,
A silken thread, where magic flows.
The stars align, in whispers sweet,
While shadows dance, and hearts compete.

Each gentle beam, a promise made,
In golden light, our fears will fade.
As night descends, our spirits soar,
In silken threads, we search for more.

The glow that calls, with tender grace,
In every glance, I see your face.
We weave our dreams, with hope's embrace,
In silver beams, we find our space.

Beneath the stars, our dreams ignite,
In every hue, there lies our light.
With each heartbeat, a song we know,
In silken warmth, our passions grow.

The night unfolds, with tales to tell,
In silken glow, we rise and swell.
Together, we, in love's sweet glow,
Embrace the night, let our hearts flow.

## Threads of Heartbeat

In every thread, a heartbeat found,
We weave the moments, love unbound.
With gentle hands, we stitch the seams,
Creating life, from thread and dreams.

As colors clash, yet blend so well,
In tangled paths, our stories tell.
A fabric rich, in hues of life,
In every knot, transcends the strife.

Through every twist, a journey made,
In threads of fate, we're never swayed.
From dawn's first pulse, to twilight's breath,
Our love endures, defying death.

With every heartbeat, stronger still,
Our threads entwined, they bend and thrill.
In tapestry, our lives embrace,
In woven dreams, we find our place.

So hold me close, in time's embrace,
In threads of heartbeat, find our grace.
Together weave, through joy and tears,
A bond that grows, through all our years.

# A Symphony of Touch

Whispers glide on fingertips,
A gentle beckoning, soft and light.
Each stroke a note, a tender kiss,
Harmony found in the heart's quiet night.

Textures speak where words fall short,
A melody born of skin's embrace.
With every caress, emotions cavort,
In the silent dance of grace.

Silken threads weave stories untold,
In the fabric of moments, close and bold.
The warmth of breaths in shared space,
Compose a score that time can't erase.

Sensation weaves its intricate ties,
A language rich with silent sighs.
Within the layers of every touch,
Lies a symphony that means so much.

Here in the quiet, hearts collide,
In the rhythm of pulses, side by side.
With every heartbeat, a tale unspools,
Creating music that endlessly rules.

# Secrets in Soft Hues

In twilight's glow, whispers arise,
Colors blend where silence sighs.
Soft pastels cradle hidden dreams,
Painting secrets in quiet streams.

Shadows dance on canvas bright,
Each stroke whispers of hidden plight.
A gentle blend of soft and bold,
Secrets of the heart silently told.

Petals open to the warmest sun,
In layers laid where time has run.
Soft hues cradle the fragile heart,
In the beauty of art, we find our part.

Each color holds a tender tale,
In every brush, our fears set sail.
The gentle whisper of dusk and dawn,
In hues of hope, we are reborn.

Lost in the beauty of fading light,
We find ourselves in the sheer delight.
In soft hues painted with care,
Our secrets linger, forever rare.

# The Language of Flesh and Paint

Fingers glide on skin so bare,
Crafting stories in the air.
A palette mixed with breaths and sighs,
In this language, the soul replies.

Canvas breathing under touch,
A world created, felt so much.
In hues of desire, passion ignites,
As time weaves through passion's flights.

Each mark a testament to the heart,
In this union, we play our part.
Textures create a visceral bond,
In flesh and paint, our spirits respond.

Colors splash in wild abandon,
In the dance of flesh, we're seldom forgotten.
A tapestry of longing, fierce, divine,
In every stroke, our bodies entwine.

Through art, through touch, we find our voice,
In the rhythm of hearts, we rejoice.
With every brush, we learn, we grow,
In the language of flesh, our truths flow.

# Dance of the Vulnerable

In the spotlight, raw and bare,
Hearts laid open, souls laid bare.
The rhythm calls, a gentle plea,
In each step, we find our key.

With every sway, the fears release,
In the dance, we find our peace.
A tapestry woven of trust and grace,
Vulnerability in this sacred space.

We move like shadows, flickering light,
In the embrace of the tranquil night.
Lines blurring, our spirits entwine,
In the dance that feels so divine.

With every turn, the world gives way,
In the dance of the vulnerable, we sway.
A fragile strength, we rise and fall,
Together we stand, together we call.

In this ballet of heart and soul,
Each step a chance to feel whole.
Through the movement, our stories told,
In the dance of the vulnerable, we are bold.

# The Tender Brush

In gentle strokes, the canvas waits,
Colors blend as magic creates.
Each hue whispers, soft and light,
A dance of shadows, day to night.

A palette rich with dreams unfurled,
Tales of love, a hidden world.
With every touch, emotions soar,
A heart revealed, forevermore.

Beneath the surface, feelings hum,
In silence, echoes softly come.
Life captured in a fleeting glance,
Art becomes our sacred dance.

Each stroke a story, pure and true,
Of moments shared, of me and you.
In every line, a breath we take,
The tender brush, our souls awake.

So let the canvas tell our tale,
With vibrant shades, we will prevail.
A masterpiece in time will thrive,
In every heart, our dreams alive.

# Veils of Presence

In shadows soft, the whispers play,
A dance of light at close of day.
Veils of presence cloak the night,
Hidden joys in muted light.

Faces blend in twilight's kiss,
Moments caught in tender bliss.
The world beyond begins to fade,
As dreams emerge from light's cascade.

Through gauzy shades, a glimpse we find,
Otherworldly, intertwined.
Each heartbeat resonates a chord,
In silence, beauty is explored.

With every breath, the night unfolds,
A tapestry of stories told.
Chasing echoes through the mist,
A sigh of love, a fleeting tryst.

In veils of presence, souls align,
A mystery, both yours and mine.
As dawn approaches, shadows fade,
Yet in the heart, the dreams we've made.

# Eyes that Speak

In silence deep, the eyes reveal,
A language pure, a spirit's feel.
With every glance, emotions flow,
Unspoken words, a timeless glow.

They dance like flames, a flickering light,
Casting warmth on the coldest night.
Each spark ignites a tale untold,
Of love and heartaches, brave and bold.

With joy and sorrow intertwined,
Eyes bring forth what hearts enshrined.
A window wide to dreams and fears,
Reflecting truths, both laughter and tears.

In crowded rooms, they seek your gaze,
A fleeting touch that sets ablaze.
In every blink, a story shared,
With eyes that speak, we're unprepared.

So look within and take your time,
For in those depths, our spirits rhyme.
With every glance, connection grows,
And in that silence, love bestows.

# Elysium of Sentiments

In realms where gentle breezes sigh,
A place where dreams no longer die.
Elysium's grace, a soft embrace,
A tapestry of love, a sacred space.

Upon the shores of tender thought,
Flowers bloom from battles fought.
Each petal, sweet, a memory bright,
In twilight's glow, all feels right.

Through whispered winds, the heart takes flight,
Spinning tales in the calm of night.
A sanctuary for hopes we keep,
In Elysium, our souls shall leap.

With every sigh, a wish is made,
In the hushed embrace of twilight's shade.
Magic lingers in every breath,
In this realm, there's no death.

So let us wander hand in hand,
In this ethereal, dreamlike land.
Where sentiments bloom and love grows free,
In Elysium, just you and me.

# Flame of Connection

In the quiet night, we twirl,
A flicker bright, love's warm swirl.
Hands clasped tight, whispers flow,
Together we ignite the glow.

With every laugh, embers dance,
In shared dreams, we take a chance.
A spark ignites, hearts entwine,
The flame of connection, so divine.

Through storms of doubt, we hold fast,
In the light, shadows are cast.
We blaze a trail through life's decree,
In the warmth of each other's decree.

The fire blooms, never wanes,
In cherished moments, joy remains.
Under stars, our souls ignite,
Together, we burn ever bright.

In the quiet night, we twirl,
A flicker bright, love's warm swirl.
Hands clasped tight, whispers flow,
The flame of connection, our sacred glow.

## Lingering Glances

Across the room, a gaze so clear,
Drawing close, yet far, my dear.
In stolen looks, a story unfolds,
A silent promise, softly told.

Moments freeze, the world falls away,
In each blink, we find our way.
Hearts race fast, breaths collide,
In lingering glances, love won't hide.

A dance of eyes, poetic art,
In your stare, I've found my heart.
Time suspends, time drips slow,
Through shared silence, passions grow.

A touch of fate, in truth, we share,
An unspoken bond, none compare.
Across the room, a gaze so clear,
Lingering glances, pulling near.

In subtle moments, feelings expand,
Two souls woven by a gentle hand.
In every glance, a world to find,
Lingering glances, heartbeats aligned.

# Carving Our Story

With tender hands, we shape the clay,
Each moment lived, a new display.
Stories etched in the heart's own skin,
Together, our journey shall begin.

In every laugh, the chisel strikes,
With memories painted, love alike.
Layers unfold, the past embraces,
In carving our story, time traces.

Through whispers shared, the canvas grows,
In the light, our affection glows.
Upon this path, together we tread,
Crafting each chapter, love unsaid.

In trials faced, we learn and grow,
Through joy and pain, our spirits flow.
With every cut, a tale is born,
In carving our story, love's adorn.

With tender hands, we shape the clay,
Each moment lived, come what may.
Stories etched in the heart's own skin,
Carving our story, together we win.

# Emotional Cartography

Maps drawn from whispers, heartbeats charted,
In every tear, our depths unguarded.
Tracing contours of joy and pain,
An emotional map, where love will reign.

With every step, new paths unfold,
Stories written in hues of gold.
We navigate through valleys and peaks,
In silent moments, our heart speaks.

Compass of feelings, guiding light,
Through shadows deep, we find our sight.
With courage bold, we explore each place,
In emotional cartography, we embrace.

Threads of laughter, stitched with care,
In every journey, the love we share.
With every heartbeat, we etch the lines,
A tapestry woven, our love defines.

Maps drawn from whispers, heartbeats charted,
The landscape vast, forever unguarded.
Through every turn, our paths align,
Emotional cartography, love's design.

# The Melody of Our Souls

In the quiet of the night, we find,
A song that stirs the heart, unconfined.
With whispers soft, like a gentle breeze,
Our spirits dance among the trees.

Notes of laughter intertwine with tears,
Echoes of hopes, dispelling fears.
Each heartbeat plays a timeless tune,
Guided by the light of the moon.

In harmony, we shape our fate,
Creating rhythms that resonate.
Together, we paint the sky so bright,
Our melody will soar in flight.

Through every trial, we won't fall,
For love's sweet song will conquer all.
Hand in hand, our voices rise,
A symphony beneath the skies.

As the final notes begin to fade,
In the silence, memories are laid.
Forever in our souls, we'll hold,
The melody, a tale retold.

# Gentle Reverberations

In twilight's hush, a whisper grows,
Soft currents where the river flows.
A tender breeze caresses me,
With gentle reverberations, I'm free.

The sunlight winks through leafy strands,
Painting shadows on the sands.
Each moment dances, light and sweet,
Echoes of life beneath our feet.

With every heartbeat, a pulse so kind,
Resonates within the mind.
Strumming notes from valleys deep,
In nature's arms, our spirits leap.

The fragrance of blossoms fills the air,
Hints of joy, beyond compare.
Every sigh a song released,
In this harmony, we find peace.

As day turns into night so good,
We gather silence like we should.
In gentle echoes, dreams arise,
Reverberations 'neath starlit skies.

# Nascent Bonds

In the garden where we first met,
Roots entwined as the sun was set.
A spark ignited, pure and rare,
In laughter shared, beyond compare.

Fledgling trust, like buds in spring,
Softly blossoming, new life to bring.
Every word, a petal's fall,
Creating magic, binding all.

With gentle steps, we paint the air,
Coloring moments, sweet and rare.
Hands joined together, heart in hand,
Building dreams, together we stand.

Through stormy skies and sunny days,
We navigate in countless ways.
This growing bond, our sacred space,
In every challenge, we find grace.

In the tapestry of time, we weave,
A story shared, we won't deceive.
With every heartbeat, we will see,
The nascent bonds that set us free.

# Underneath the Surface

Beneath the calm, a storm does brew,
Whispers of depth that few pursue.
Veiled mysteries in shadows dim,
The currents pull, they draw us in.

Secrets hidden, waiting to rise,
In the stillness, truth belies.
Each wave a story, lost to time,
In depths where silence seeks to rhyme.

With every ripple, the heart feels bold,
As emotions surface, stories unfold.
We dive deep, embrace the unknown,
In the depth of our hearts, we have grown.

In pools of longing, we find our way,
Tracing paths where shadows play.
The depth, a mirror reflecting the soul,
In unveiling truths, we become whole.

So let us plunge, unafraid to see,
The beauty that blooms in the dark sea.
Underneath the surface, we'll find,
The treasure that nourishes the mind.

Milton Keynes UK
Ingram Content Group UK Ltd.
UKHW052022251024
450245UK00012B/643

9 789916 891797